ACTIVITY WEATHER BOOKS FOR KIDS AGES 4-8

All About Weather-Fun Early Learning

Mark Steven

D1711744

THE WEATHER

AUTUMN

September   October   November

Choose the correct answer. ?

NATURE   FRUIT   ANIMALS   CLOTHES   WEATHER

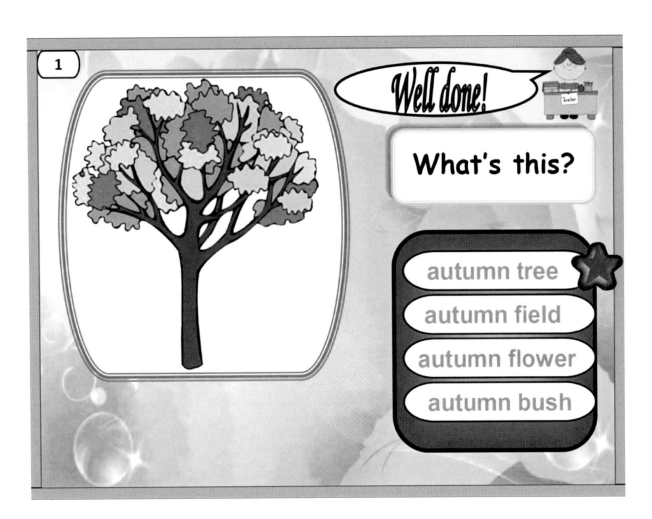

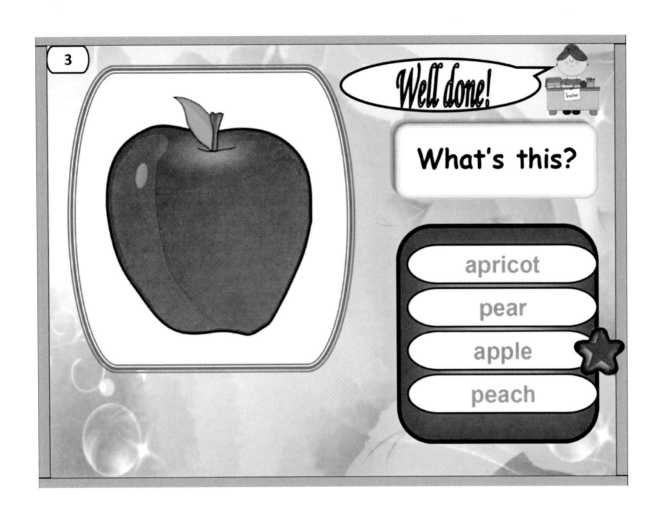

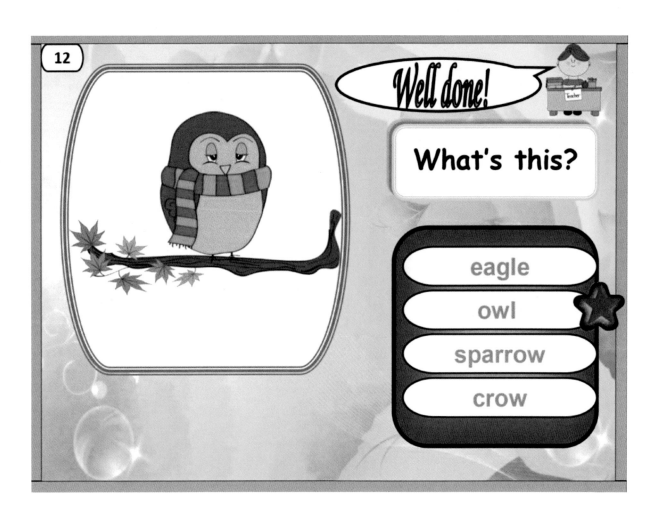

16

Well done!

What do we need in autumn?

- sunshade
- umbrella
- sundial
- flip-flops

What is he doing?

He is snowboarding.

He is skiing.

He is sledging.

What is he doing?

He is making
a snowman.

He is making
a snow angel.

They are having
a snowball fight.

He is snowboarding.

He is making a snow angel.

He is sledging.

What are they doing?

They are making a snow castle.

They are making a snow angel.

They are making a snowman.

What are they doing?

They are racing horses.

They are riding a horse.

They are riding in a one-horse open sleigh.

What is she doing?

She is skiing.

She is sledging.

She is skating.

He is cross-country skiing.

He is rollerblading.

He is snowboarding.

What are they doing? 13

They are
speed-skating.

They are making
a snow angel.

They playing
ice-hockey.

What is he doing?

He is snowboarding.

He is skateboarding.

He is skiing.

What is he doing?

He is snowboarding.

He is shovelling snow.

He is playing ice-hockey.

The Answers

1- He is skiing.   2- He is skating.   3- They are having a snowball fight.

4- He is making a snow castle. 5- He is making a snow angel.

6- They are making a snowman. 7- They are riding in a one-horse open sleigh. 8- She is sledging. 9- He is cross-country skiing. 10 Curling

11- He is ice fishing. 12- Biathlon . 13- They are

14- playing ice-hockey. 15- He is snowboarding.

16- He is shovelling snow.

How's the weather?

 It's Monday.

Look at Sarah and Tom!

How's the weather?

 It's cloudy and rainy!

 It's Tuesday.

Look at Sarah and Tom!

How's the weather?

It's windy!

It's foggy!

 It's Thursday.

Look at Sarah!
How's the weather?

It's cold!

It's Friday.

Look at Sarah and Tom!
How's the weather?

It's snowy and very cold!

It's Saturday.

Look at Jane and John!

How's the weather?

It's Sunday.

Look at Jane and John!

How's the weather?

It's sunny and very hot!

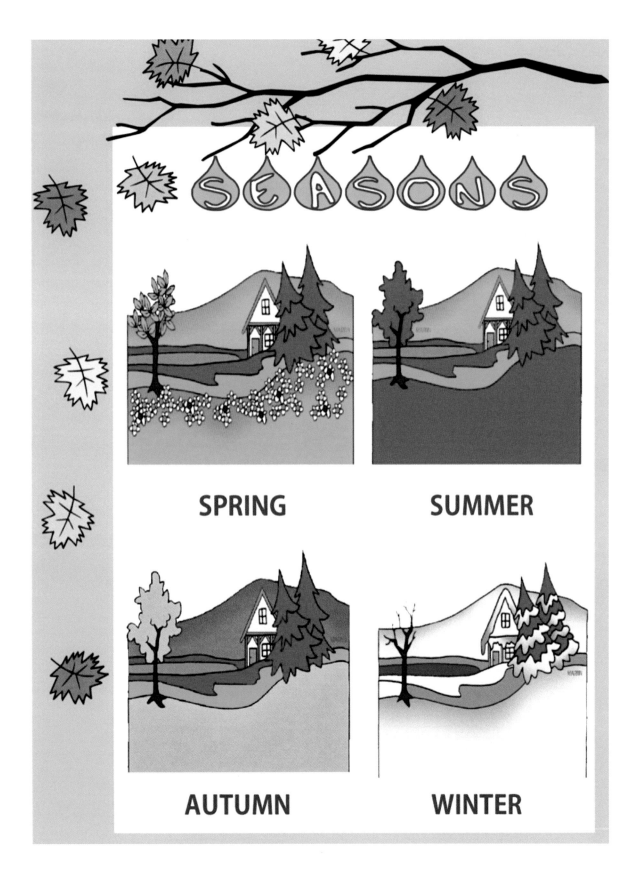

SPRING

In spring

-it is warm.
-it is nice
-people go outside
for a walk.
-flowers bloom.

SUMMER

In summer

-it is hot.
-it is sunny.
-people go to the
beach.
-people usually go
on holiday.

AUTUMN/FALL

In autumn

-it is often windy.
-it is cloudy.
-it rains = it is rainy.
-it is a bit cold.

SUMMER

In summer

-it is hot.
-it is sunny.
-people go to the beach.
-people usually go on holiday.

Weather

rain · stars · moon · sun · thunder · snow · tornado · crescent · snowflakes · rainbow

Hurry up!

It's raining.

I'm wet.

Let's review!

Hurry up!

It's raining.

I'm wet.

Let's write!

I'<u>m</u> wet.

I<u>t</u>'s raining.

Hurry up

What's the Weather Like?

It's Sunny

It's sunny.

It's sunny.

I'm hot.

I'm hot.

Let's write!

I'<u>m</u> hot.

It's _sunny.

H u_rry u_p

It's snowing.

I'm cold.

It's snowing

I'm cold.

Let's write!

It's snow**i**ng

I'm col_d

Made in the USA
Coppell, TX
21 March 2020